THE OLYMPIC GAMES

Ron Thomas & Jan Hipgrave

M

Acknowledgements

The author and publishers are grateful to the following for permission to reproduce photographs and copyright material:
Australian Picture Library, pp. 1, 4, 15, 16;
Stock Photos, pp. 24, 28;
UPI (United Press International), p. 27;
Cover photographs © Tony Duffy
© Steve Powell
ALL-SPORT AUSTRALIA

Design and illustration by Stephen Pascoe

First published 1988 (Reprinted 1988)
Second edition published 1992 by
MACMILLAN EDUCATION AUSTRALIA PTY LTD
107 Moray Street, South Melbourne 3205
6 Clarke Street, Crows Nest 2065

Associated companies and representatives throughout the world

National Library of Australia
cataloguing in publication data

Thomas, Ron, 1947 –
The Olympic Games.

Includes index.
ISBN 0 7329 1360 8

1. Olympic games — Juvenile literature. I. Hipgrave, Jan. II. Title.

796.4′8

Set in Souvenir by Superskill Graphics, Singapore
Printed in Hong Kong

Contents

An Olympic torchbearer.

Foot race at the first Olympics.

The First Olympic Games

The ancient Greeks believed that Mount Olympus, behind Olympia, was the home of their gods.

The first Olympic Games were held in 776 B.C. They were held in Ancient Greece at a place called Olympia.
At these first Games foot races were held in honour of Zeus, the king of the Greek gods.

Ancient Events

A few years after the first Olympic Games, the athletes competed in throwing, jumping and wrestling events as well as the running races. Only Greek men were allowed to compete. No slaves were allowed to enter the events and women were forbidden to even watch.
Some women did enter events. They disguised themselves and competed but whenever they were caught they were killed.

In 264 B.C. a woman was allowed to enter a chariot race. She won!

Discus thrower.

The Games at Olympia

Our word Stadium comes from the Greek word 'stadion' which means a foot race of about 200 metres.

At Olympia, a stadium was built where people went to watch the track and field events.
A hippodrome was built for chariot races. The athletes and their coaches lived in a gymnasium nearby where they trained and prepared for the games.
Athletes came from all parts of Greece.
The time of the Games was a time of peace and friendship.
Every athlete had to take an oath to play fairly and be a good sportsman.
The Games were held every four years for more than 1000 years.

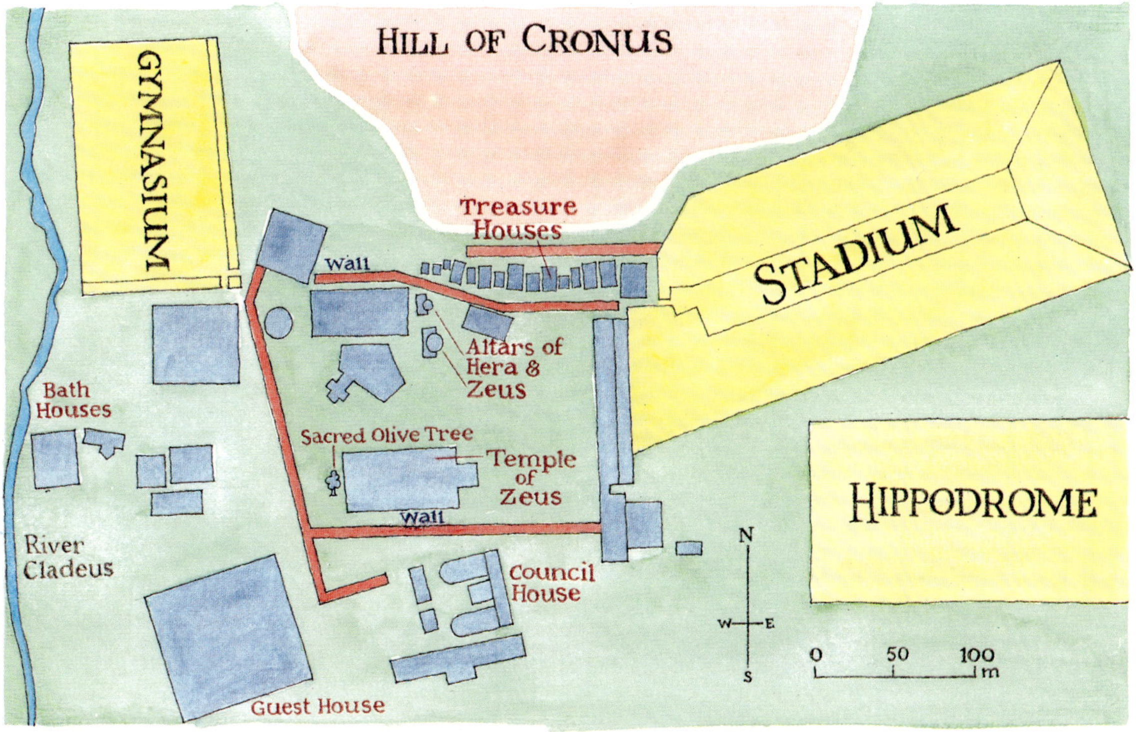

ANCIENT OLYMPIA

An ancient wrestling event.

The End of the Ancient Olympics

After the Romans conquered Greece, the Olympic Oath became forgotten. Competitors often cheated.
In A.D. 394 the Roman Emperor Theodosius stopped the Games.
The Olympic Games were forgotten for over 1500 years.

The four year period between Games was, and still is, known as an Olympiad.

How Ancient Olympia was found

In 1875 a group of German archaeologists were digging in Greece.
Beneath rocks and sand they discovered the ruins of the ancient town of Olympia with its stadium, hippodrome and gymnasium.
People all around the world heard about the ancient Olympic Games.

Archaeologists digging up Olympia.

Baron Pierre de Coubertin.

The Olympic Games Reborn

It was a Frenchman, Baron Pierre de Coubertin, who thought that it would be a good idea to hold Olympic Games again.
He liked the idea of athletes from all countries competing in a friendly competition.
So in 1894 he arranged a meeting of people from nine countries to talk about his idea.
This group became the first International Olympic Committee.

The 1896 Olympic Games

Winners were awarded an olive branch and a gold medal while runners-up received a branch of laurel leaves and a bronze medal.

Two years after this meeting, in 1896, the first modern Olympic Games were held in Athens, Greece.

Only 311 competitors took part.

At these first Games the events were Athletics, Gymnastics, Water sports, Horse-riding events, Fighting sports, Cycling and Weightlifting.

Women were not allowed to enter the 1896 Olympic Games.

This rule was changed for the next Olympics in Paris in 1900.

Athletes at the 1896 Games.

The Modern Olympic Message

Baron de Coubertin said:

> "The most important thing in the Olympic Games is not to win but to take part. Just as the most important thing in life is not the triumph but the struggle."

Australia, Greece, Britain and Switzerland are the only countries to have sent athletes to every modern Olympic Games.

These words have been displayed on the scoreboard at every modern Olympic Games since 1896.

The International Olympic Committee (IOC)

Since the first modern Olympic Games the IOC has been the organiser of the Games. It is this Committee which says which sports will be in the Games and it sets the rules of the competition.
The International Olympic Committee decides in which country the Games will be held.
Areas in which Summer and Winter Olympics have been held are shown on the map below, and listed on page 31.

Host countries of the Summer and Winter Olympics.

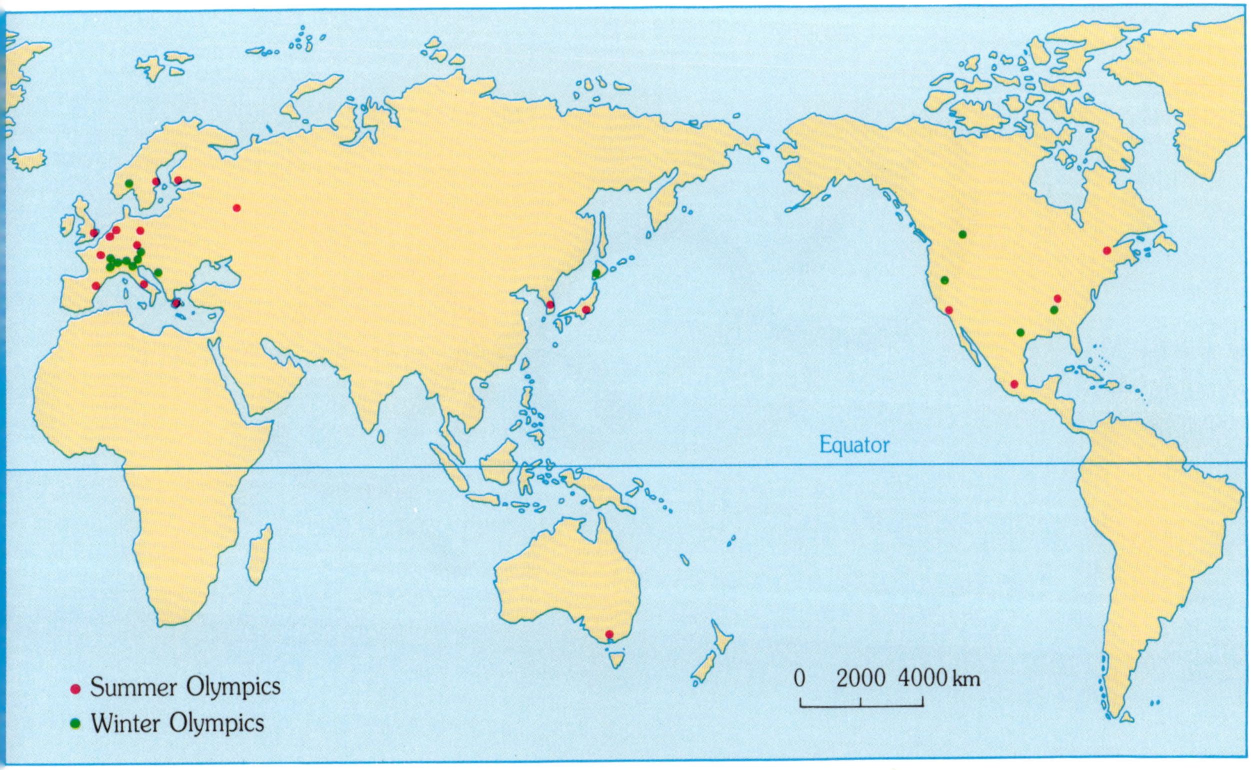

The Olympic Flag

Baron de Coubertin designed the Olympic symbol of five intertwining coloured rings.
The colours are blue, green, red, yellow and black.
The colours were chosen because at least one of them is used in the flags of every country in the world.
The coloured rings are on a white flag.
The flag was first used at the Games in 1920 and is flown throughout the Olympic Games.

The Olympic Motto is written in Latin and means "Swifter, Higher, Stronger."

The Olympic Flame

The Olympic Flame was first used at the modern Olympic Games in 1928 at Amsterdam, in the Netherlands.

Before the start of each Olympic Games the Olympic Torch is lit at Olympia in Greece, the site of the ancient Olympics.
It is then carried by many runners to the host city.
This is like a long relay race through many countries of the world.
The last runner, carrying the torch, runs into the main stadium at the time of the Opening Ceremony.
The Olympic Flame is then lit.
It burns throughout the Games and is only put out at the Closing Ceremony.

The Opening Ceremony

Into the main stadium, crowded with spectators, march the athletes from all the competing countries.
Ahead of each team one member carries each nation's flag.
The teams enter the arena in alphabetical order, except Greece which always leads (because the Olympic Games originated in that country), and the host country's team which enters last.
The Head of State of the host country, for example, the President, the King, the Queen, or the Governor-General, declares the Games open.

The release of doves became an official part of the Opening Ceremony in 1920.

Opening Ceremony, Los Angeles, 1984.

The Olympic Flag is then brought into the arena and raised on the flagpole. It will remain fluttering above the crowd until the Closing Ceremony.
The Olympic Torch arrives all the way from Greece, and the Olympic Flame is lit.
One athlete from the host country says the Olympic Oath on behalf of all the athletes. The oath is a pledge to obey the rules.
Following the Opening there is a great entertainment spectacle with dancing, songs and music. Thousands of doves are released as a symbol of peace.

The Athletes' Oath

The judges also take an oath pledging fair play.

Just as the ancient Greek athletes had to swear an oath to play fairly, so do the competitors in the modern Olympic Games.
Baron de Coubertin wrote the Athletes' Oath.

> "In the name of all competitors, I promise that we will take part in these Olympic Games, respecting and abiding by all the rules which govern them in the true spirit of sportsmanship, for the glory of sport and the honour of our teams."

This vow is made at the Opening Ceremony of the Olympic Games.

Modern Olympic Events

The events open to Olympic competition at the Barcelona Olympic Games are:

- ARCHERY
- ATHLETICS
- BADMINTON
- BASEBALL
- BASKETBALL
- BOXING
- CANOEING
- CYCLING
- EQUESTRIAN SPORTS
- FENCING
- FOOTBALL
- GYMNASTICS
- HANDBALL
- HOCKEY
- JUDO
- MODERN PENTATHLON
- ROWING
- SHOOTING
- SWIMMING
  - SWIMMING
  - DIVING
  - SYNCHRONISED
  - WATERPOLO
- TABLE TENNIS
- TENNIS
- VOLLEYBALL
- WEIGHTLIFTING
- WRESTLING
- YACHTING

Demonstration Sports

At every Olympic Games there are some new sports. These are called demonstration sports. At the 1992 Games, these are Roller Hockey, Pelota and Taekwondo.

Taekwondo

Pelota

Roller Hockey

High jump.

Decathlon

The Decathlon is for men only. It's an Athletics event.
There are 10 events. Competitors score points for how well they do in each event.
The 10 events are:

- 100 METRE RUN
- LONG JUMP
- SHOT-PUT
- HIGH JUMP
- 400 METRE RUN
- 110 METRE HURDLES
- DISCUS
- POLE VAULT
- JAVELIN
- 1500 METRE RUN

The Tug-of-War was an Olympic event between 1900–1924.

A javelin thrower.

Heptathlon

The Heptathlon is for women only. It's an Athletics event. It was first included in 1984. The events are:

- 100 METRE HURDLES
- LONG JUMP
- SHOT-PUT
- JAVELIN
- 800 METRE RUN
- HIGH JUMP
- 200 METRE RUN

The Heptathlon takes the place of the women's Pentathlon which was a contest of five events.

Modern Pentathlon

The Modern Pentathlon is a contest of five events for men only. It was thought of by Baron de Coubertin in 1912.
The events are:

- HORSE RIDING
- FENCING
- CROSS-COUNTRY RUN
- PISTOL SHOOT
- SWIMMING

An equestrian.

Marathon

In 1984 a Marathon race for women was introduced into the Olympic Games.

The Marathon is a 42 kilometre run.
The start and finish are usually in the main arena.
The rest of the race is run on the roads of the city and takes between two and three hours.
The Marathon is run to remember a Greek who ran from a town called Marathon to Athens with the news that a battle at Marathon against the Persians had been won.
This happened over 2500 years ago.

A Marathon runner.

The gold medal is awarded to the athlete who comes first in the final of an event.

Medals

The athletes who come First, Second or Third in the final of each event receive a medal.
The medal for first place is made of silver but is covered with gold.
The second place winner is given a silver medal and the third place medal is made of bronze.

Medal Ceremony

The three medal winners stand on a podium and are given their medals.
They stand to attention while the national anthem of the winner's country is played.
The flags of the three medal winners are raised.

Gold medals were first given in 1908.

Coaching an athlete.

Training for the Olympics

Athletes must train hard. They practise every day for many hours. They still have to work or go to school as well.
Each athlete has a coach who teaches them and plans their training.
An Olympic athlete must be an 'AMATEUR'. This means that an athlete cannot be paid for being a coach or for competing in athletics.
Every country has a committee to choose the athletes for the Games. Trials are held and the best athletes are chosen.

Troubles at the Olympics

The spirit of the Olympic Games is that athletes compete in friendly and peaceful games.
Sometimes this has not happened.
In 1916, 1940 and 1944 the Games were not held because of the two World Wars.
In more recent years some countries have used the Olympic Games to show their dislike of other countries.
In 1972 at the Munich Games some members of Israel's team were killed by terrorists.
In 1980 the United States boycotted (didn't go to) the Moscow Games.
In 1984 Russia stayed away from the Los Angeles Games.

Protesters for a peaceful Games.

Winter Olympics

In 1984, Ice Dancing was included as a sport in the Winter Olympics.

The Winter Olympics began in 1924 and were first held in France.
The International Olympic Committee (IOC) is in charge of the Winter Olympics. The Committee chooses the sports to be included in the Games, sets the rules and selects which country will host the Winter Olympics.
The Winter Olympics are held every four years too. They were held in the same year as the Summer Olympic Games until 1992.
From 1994 they will be held every four years. This means that they will no longer be held in the same year as the Summer Olympics.

1992	Summer Olympics	Barcelona, Spain
1992	Winter Olympics	Albertville, France
1994	Winter Olympics	Lillehammer, Norway
1996	Summer Olympics	Atlanta, USA

Winter sports events are chosen from:

- BIATHLON (SHOOTING AND CROSS-COUNTRY SKIING)
- BOBSLED
- FIGURE SKATING
- ICE DANCING
- ICE HOCKEY
- SPEED SKATING
- SKI JUMP
- SKIING — ALPINE AND NORDIC
- LUGE (SLEDDING)

Paralympics

The 'Paralympics' are international games held for the physically disabled.
They are held in the same year as the Olympic Games and are usually held in the same country.
The Paralympics were first held in Rome in 1960.
All countries can send representatives to compete.
Events are chosen from:

- ARCHERY
- BASKETBALL
- SHOOTING
- SNOOKER
- SHOT-PUT
- DISCUS
- JAVELIN
- TABLE TENNIS
- LAWN BOWLS
- SWIMMING
- WHEELCHAIR RACES
- MARATHON
- WEIGHTLIFTING
- SLALOM RACES

Spain

Spain is a country in Europe.
The capital city is Madrid. Barcelona is another big city in Spain, and this is where the 1992 summer Olympics will be held.
In Spain the weather is sunny and warm in summer.
The language spoken is Spanish.
The money is called the peseta.
The Spaniards like to eat paella which is seafood and rice. Another famous dish is gazpacho. It's a cold tomato soup.
There is a royal family in Spain, headed by the King.
The country is run by a government led by the Prime Minister.

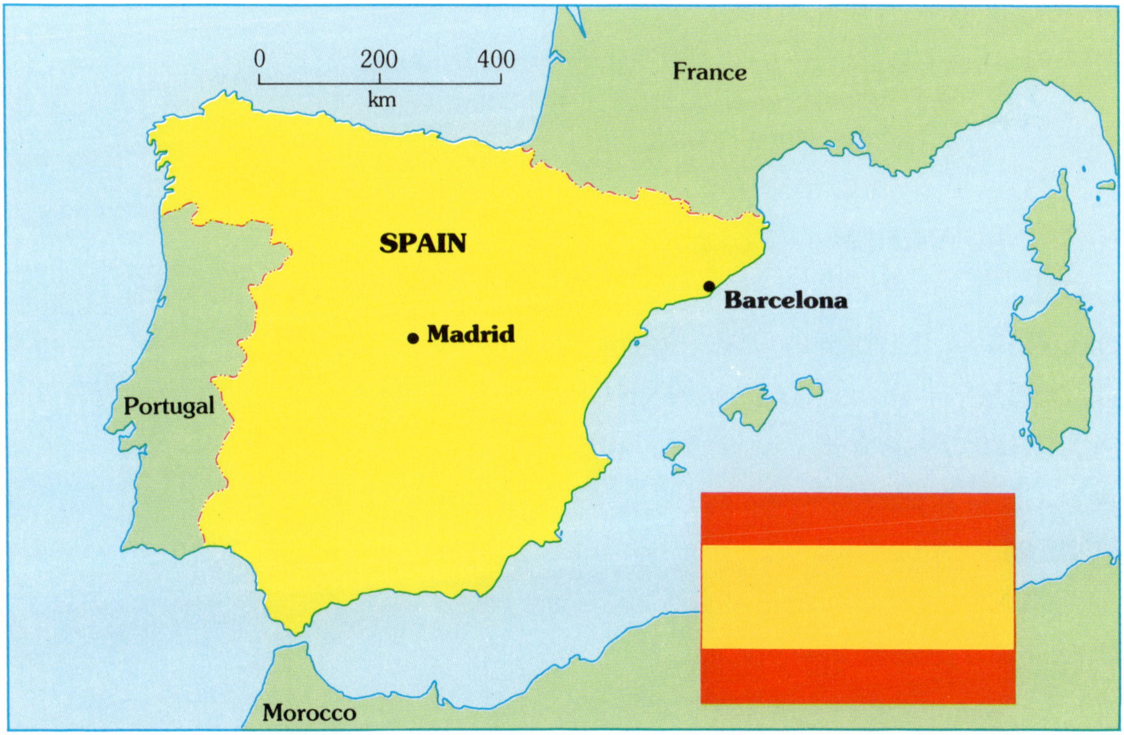

Glossary

AMATEUR — Someone who competes or coaches without pay.

ATHLETE — A person who competes in sports.

B.C. — The years before the birth of Christ.

BIATHLON — A winter Olympic event combining shooting and cross-country skiing.

BOYCOTT — To stay away in protest.

BRONZE — A metal made of copper and tin.

COACH — An instructor and helper.

DECATHLON — A contest made up of 10 separate track and field events for men.

GYMNASIUM — A building for exercising.

HEPTATHLON — A contest made up of 7 separate track and field events for women.

HIPPODROME — An arena for chariot racing.

HOST CITY — The city where the Olympic Games are held.

MARATHON — A 42 kilometre race.

MEDAL — A token of success. An Olympic medal is round, made of gold, silver or bronze, and hangs on a rope around the winner's neck.

MOTTO — A short saying.

NATIONAL ANTHEM — A country's official song.

OATH — A promise.

OLYMPIA — The town in Greece where the Olympics began.

OLYMPIAD — The four years between Olympic Games.

PENTATHLON — A contest made up of 5 events.

PLEDGE — A promise.

PODIUM — A platform.

STADIUM — A place where athletic events are held.

VOW — To promise.

ZEUS - King of the ancient Greek gods.

Facts and Figures

HOST CITIES OF THE MODERN OLYMPIC GAMES

Year	Summer Olympics	Winter Olympics
1896	Athens, Greece	
1900	Paris, France	
1904	St. Louis, Missouri, USA	
1908	London, England	
1912	Stockholm, Sweden	
1916	Not held because of World War I	
1920	Antwerp, Belgium	
1924	Paris, France	Chamonix, France
1928	Amsterdam, The Netherlands	St. Moritz, Switzerland
1932	Los Angeles, California, USA	Lake Placid, New York, USA
1936	Berlin, Germany	Garmisch-Partenkirchen, Germany
1940	Not held because of World War II	
1944	Not held because of World War II	
1948	London, England	St. Moritz, Switzerland
1952	Helsinki, Finland	Oslo, Norway
1956	Melbourne, Australia	Cortina, Italy
1960	Rome, Italy	Squaw Valley, California, USA
1964	Tokyo, Japan	Innsbruck, Austria
1968	Mexico City, Mexico	Grenoble, France
1972	Munich, West Germany	Sapporo, Japan
1976	Montreal, Canada	Innsbruck, Austria
1980	Moscow, Russia	Lake Placid, New York
1984	Los Angeles, California, USA	Sarajevo, Yugoslavia (1984)
1988	Seoul, Korea	Calgary, Alberta, Canada
1992	Barcelona, Spain	Albertville, France
1996	Atlanta, USA	Lillehammer, Norway (1994)

MEDAL WINNERS

Most Gold Medals

Men: Ray Ewry (Standing Jumps in 3 Olympics) 10 medals.
Women: Larissa Latynina (Gymnast) 9 medals.

Most Medals

Men: Nikolai Andrianov (Gymnast) 15 medals.
Women: Larissa Latynina (Gymnast) 18 medals.

Index